WHS

practise

Mental Maths

9-10

YEARS

Key Stage 2

Test 1

A 1 $4\overline{)28}$

2 $15 \times 10 =$

3 What is 50% of £20.00?

4 £1.50 – £0.50 =

5 What is the perimeter of this shape?

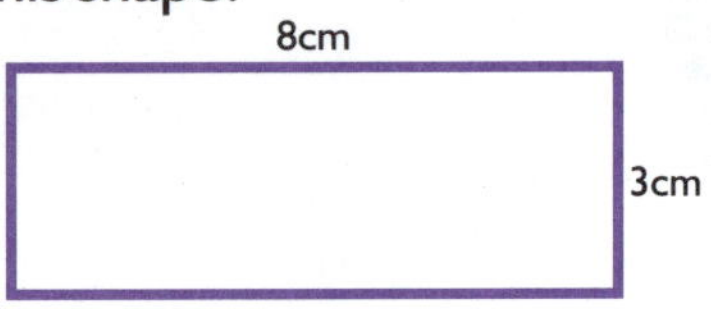

B 1 Multiply £8 by 8.

2 £4.00 – £1.50 =

3 Multiply 17 by 10.

4 Divide 41 by 8.

5 How much is two-thirds of 27p?

C 1 A number divided by 10 is 26. What is the number?

2 What is the total of £3.20 and £4.60?

3 How much is 75% of 28?

4 Divide 600 by 10.

5 Take £2.50 from £4.70.

Test 2

A 1 $23 + 10 =$

2 What is the perimeter of this shape?

3 $6 \times 6 =$

4 40p + 35p =

5 How much is $\frac{1}{2}$ of 40?

B 1 How much change do you get from £5 if you buy something for £1.95?

2 $18 \times 100 =$

3 Add 46cm and 54cm.

4 $8 \times 7 =$

5 What is half of 80?

C 1 If 7 oranges cost 56p how much will 5 oranges cost?

2 Divide £6.50 by 50.

3 How many grams in 2.5kg?

4 What is the area of a square with sides 12cm long?

5 What is three-quarters of 80?

Helpful hints

It is useful to be able to work out sums to do with money in our heads.

Here is how to work out how much change we need when buying something.

Example: buying something for £3.65 with a £5 note.

1 Add on 5p to make £3.70.

2 Add on 30p to make £4.00.

3 Add on £1 to make £5.00.

We have added on 5p + 30p + £1 which is £1.35 so that is the change we should receive.

The hard part is remembering what you add on as you go but it gets easier with practice.

Second example: paying for something costing £2.32 with a £10 note.

1 Add on 8p to make £2.40.

2 Add on 60p to make £3.00.

3 Add on £7.00 to make £10.00.

We have added 8p + 60p + £7.00 which is £7.68 so that is the change we should receive.

Test 3

A How much change do you get if you:

1 pay with a £5 note for something costing £2.60? ______

2 pay with a £5 note for something costing £3.40? ______

3 buy something for £1.80 with two £1 coins? ______

4 buy something for £3.10 with four £1 coins? ______

B How much change do you get if you:

1 pay with a £5 note for something costing £1.75? ______

2 pay with a £10 note for something costing £6.35? ______

3 pay with a £5 note for something costing 85p? ______

4 buy something costing £7.25 with a £10 note? ______

C How much change do you get if you:

1 pay with a £5 note for something costing £1.73? ______

2 pay with a £5 note for something costing £3.51? ______

3 pay with a £10 note for something costing £5.09? ______

4 buy something costing £1.42 with a £10 note? ______

Test 4

A 1 $56 + 20 =$ ______

2 $6 \times \frac{1}{2} =$ ______

3 $4\overline{)24}$ ______

4 $10 \times 10 =$ ______

5 What is the perimeter of this rectangle? ______

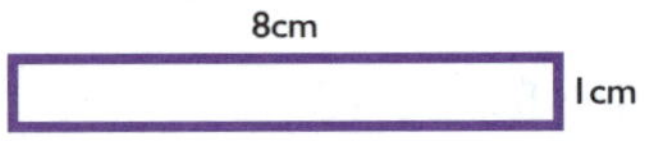

B 1 $9 \times 9 =$ ______

2 How much change do you get from £5 if you buy something costing £1.25? ______

3 What is 25% of £28? ______

4 $32 \times 100 =$ ______

5 Divide 400 by 10. ______

C 1 If 9 bananas cost 63p how much will 4 bananas cost? ______

2 How many hours are there in 3 days? ______

3 What is the mode of these numbers?
5, 10, 5, 15, 15, 10, 5, 15, 5 ______

4 What is 75% of £8.00? ______

5 What is the area of a rectangle 4cm long and $6\frac{1}{2}$ cm wide? ______

Test 5

A 1 $4\overline{)28}$ ______

2 $14 \times 10 =$ ______

3 How many minutes are there between 3:45 and 4:25? ______

4 How much change do you get from £5 if you buy something costing £4.20? ______

5 $35 + 40 =$ ______

B 1 What is 25% of £20? ______

2 If 8 apples cost 64p, how much will 1 apple cost? ______

3 What is a quarter of 80? ______

4 Multiply 7 by 6. ______

5 What is the perimeter of a rectangle with sides 2.5cm and 3.5cm? ______

C 1 How much change do you get from £10 if you buy something costing £4.22? ______

2 Divide £20 by 8. ______

3 Write all the factors of 18. ______

4 What is the mode of this list?
2, 6, 8, 3, 7, 2, 9, 4 ______

5 Which number comes next?
2, 4, 8, 16, ______

Challenge 1

1 Tasha thinks of a number then doubles the number and adds 6. Her answer is 18.
What number did she begin with? ______

2 Joe thinks of a number then multiplies it by 9, then takes away 7. His answer is 47.
What number did Joe start with? ______

3 Patrick thinks of a fairly large number then doubles it and then takes away 30. His answer is 170.
What number did Patrick start with? ______

4 Renuka multiplies a number by 3 and then divides it by 2.
Her answer is 12. What was the number? ______

5 Tom multiplies a number by itself and then adds 20 to it. The answer is 69. What was the number? ______

6 Tuhil multiplies a number by itself and then multiplies the answer by the first number again. The final number is 64.
What number did Tuhil start with? ______

7 Duncan divides a number by 2 and then adds 20.
His answer is 520. What was the number? ______

8 Verity takes 6 from a number, multiplies the new number by 2 and has the answer 52.
What was her starting number? ______

Test 6

A 1 $10\overline{)30}$

2 How much change do you get from three £1 coins if you buy something costing £2.80?

3 What is 50% of £5?

4 $8 \times 5 =$

5 £1.30 + £1.40 =

B 1 What is 25% of 4?

2 6 packets of paper cost £36.00. How much will 1 packet cost?

3 Add 35, 25 and 10.

4 A rectangle has a perimeter of 14cm. One side is 3cm, how long is the second side?

5 Multiply £50 by 100.

C 1 What change do you get from £20 when you buy something for £8.31?

2 £3.20 – £1.40 =

3 Which number comes next?

1, 10, 100, ____

4 A square has an area of $25cm^2$. What is the length of the sides?

5 Write all the factors of 20.

Test 7

A 1 Add 6, 7 and 8.

2 $20 \times 10 =$

3 What is the perimeter of this square?

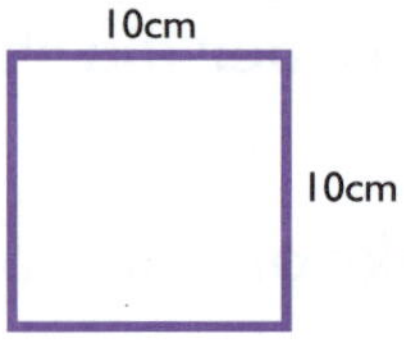

4 $6 \times 5 =$

5 $10\overline{)90}$

B 1 What is $\frac{1}{3}$ of 12?

2 Divide 36 by 9.

3 £4.00 + £2.67 =

4 What change do you get from four £1 coins if you buy something costing £3.45?

5 Half of a number is 26. What is the number?

C 1 10 tape measures cost £65. How much does 1 tape cost?

2 £4.00 – £2.75 =

3 Add 31cm, 17cm and 20cm.

4 A rectangle has an area of $54cm^2$. One side is 6cm. How long is the second side?

5 How many 10p pieces are the same as £9.20?

Helpful hints

When we multiply decimals by 10 or 100 it is useful to have a rough (approximate) idea of the size of the answer as it helps us to see if our answer is correct.

Example: 3.7 × 100

First, we know that 3.7 is just under 4. Second, we know that 4 × 100 is 400 so our answer should be a bit under 400. If our answer is nowhere near 400 our answer must be wrong. The correct answer is 370.0.

Example:
Do you think this answer is correct?
4.9 × 100 = 49.0

First, we know that 4.9 is a little less than 5. Second, we know that 5 × 100 is 500, so 49.0 is **not** a sensible answer. We know we have done something wrong. The answer should be 490.0.

A 1 6.0 × 10 = ______
2 9.0 × 10 = ______
3 3.0 × 10 = ______
4 4.5 × 10 = ______
5 7.5 × 10 = ______

B 1 3.1 × 100 = ______
2 5.8 × 100 = ______
3 12.5 × 10 = ______
4 21.2 × 10 = ______
5 10.2 × 10 = ______

C 1 13.6 × 100 = ______
2 0.8 × 100 = ______
3 42.2 × 10 = ______
4 0.2 × 10 = ______
5 130.2 × 100 = ______

Challenge 2

You should be able to work out these sums in your head.
Add a number to column 1 to make the answer in column 3.
Write your answer in column 2.

Column 1	Column 2	Column 3
2.6	1.3	3.9
3.2		5.7
1.8		4.6
4.6		9.8
3.4		5.2
9.5		9.8
4.6		7.3
5.4		9.1
3.7		7.6
6.2		8.1

Test 9

A 1 $3.0 \times 10 =$ ______

2 $4 \times 5 =$ ______

3 What is $\frac{1}{2}$ of 12? ______

4 £2.00 + £3.00 = ______

5 $18 - 7 =$ ______

B 1 What is $\frac{1}{4}$ of 24? ______

2 $6.9 \times 10 =$ ______

3 £3.50 + £1.20 = ______

4 $26 - 17 =$ ______

5 $9 \times 9 =$ ______

C 1 Multiply 8 by 8. ______

2 What is $\frac{2}{3}$ of 18? ______

3 $0.6 \times 100 =$ ______

4 What is the change from £5 if you spend £1.72? ______

5 £2.30 + £3.35 = ______

Test 10

A 1 What is $\frac{1}{2}$ of 6? ______

2 $3 \times 8 =$ ______

3 $15 - 6 =$ ______

4 $4.0 \times 10 =$ ______

5 £6.00 – £2.00 = ______

B 1 $23 - 9 =$ ______

2 $7 \times 6 =$ ______

3 What is $\frac{1}{4}$ of 32? ______

4 $7.1 \times 100 =$ ______

5 £5.00 – £1.30 = ______

C 1 £2.00 – £1.28 = ______

2 Multiply 7p by 8. ______

3 What is $\frac{2}{3}$ of 21? ______

4 What is the change from £20 if you spend £14.67? ______

5 $1.1 \times 10 =$ ______

Test 11

A 1 What is $\frac{1}{2}$ of £1.00? ________

2 3.0 × 10 = ________

3 £4.50 + £2.00 = ________

4 13 – 8 = ________

5 3 × 5 = ________

B 1 What is $\frac{1}{4}$ of 36? ________

2 5.8 × 10 = ________

3 £6.50 + £2.20 = ________

4 Multiply 9 by 2. ________

5 33 – 12 = ________

C 1 Multiply 36.1 by 100. ________

2 What is one-fifth ($\frac{1}{5}$) of 25? ________

3 £1.63 + £0.28 = ________

4 Multiply £12 by 3. ________

5 What is the change from £10 if you spend £8.13? ________

Test 12

A 1 £3.00 – £1.50 = ________

2 2 × 8 = ________

3 What is $\frac{1}{2}$ of 1 metre? ________

4 8.0 × 100 = ________

5 15 – 9 = ________

B 1 Multiply 7 by 3. ________

2 30 – 11 = ________

3 4.9 × 100 = ________

4 How much is a quarter of 28? ________

5 £3.80 – £1.20 = ________

C 1 What is one-fifth ($\frac{1}{5}$) of 10? ________

2 What is the change from £10 if you spend £7.08? ________

3 Multiply 60.2 by 10. ________

4 £3.20 – £1.65 = ________

5 Multiply £15 by 2. ________

Test 13

A 1 $2 \times 8 =$ ______

2 $14 \times \frac{1}{2} =$ ______

3 £3.05 + £2.50 = ______

4 $1.0 \times 100 =$ ______

5 $14 - 7 =$ ______

B 1 £1.30 + £1.45 = ______

2 Multiply 8.7 by 10. ______

3 How many ml are there in 0.5 litre? ______

4 Multiply 10 by 7. ______

5 $31 - 9 =$ ______

C 1 A number divided by 8 gives the answer 6. What is the number? ______

2 How much is one-fifth ($\frac{1}{5}$) of £1.00? ______

3 £2.64 + £1.26 = ______

4 If 4 eggs cost 48p, how much will 2 eggs cost? ______

5 What is 100 times 30.3? ______

Test 14

A 1 £4.00 – £1.50 = ______

2 $20 \times \frac{1}{2} =$ ______

3 $5.0 \times 10 =$ ______

4 $3 \times 7 =$ ______

5 $11 - 6 =$ ______

B 1 Multiply 6 by 8. ______

2 How much is $\frac{1}{2}$ of £3.00? ______

3 $34 - 15 =$ ______

4 £4.00 – £1.70 = ______

5 Multiply 12.2 by 10. ______

C 1 £4.00 – £1.38 = ______

2 If 5 oranges cost 55p, how much will 8 oranges cost? ______

3 Multiply 6.2 cm by 100. ______

4 How much is one-fifth ($\frac{1}{5}$) of 2 metres? ______

5 A number divided by 6 gives the answer 7. What is the number? ______

Challenge 3

The factors of number 9 are 1, 3 and 9.
Look at the numbers below and write all their factors in the boxes.

6

10

18

21

29

36

42

49

55

80

Challenge 4

Put the sums in the circles that correctly represent the answers.

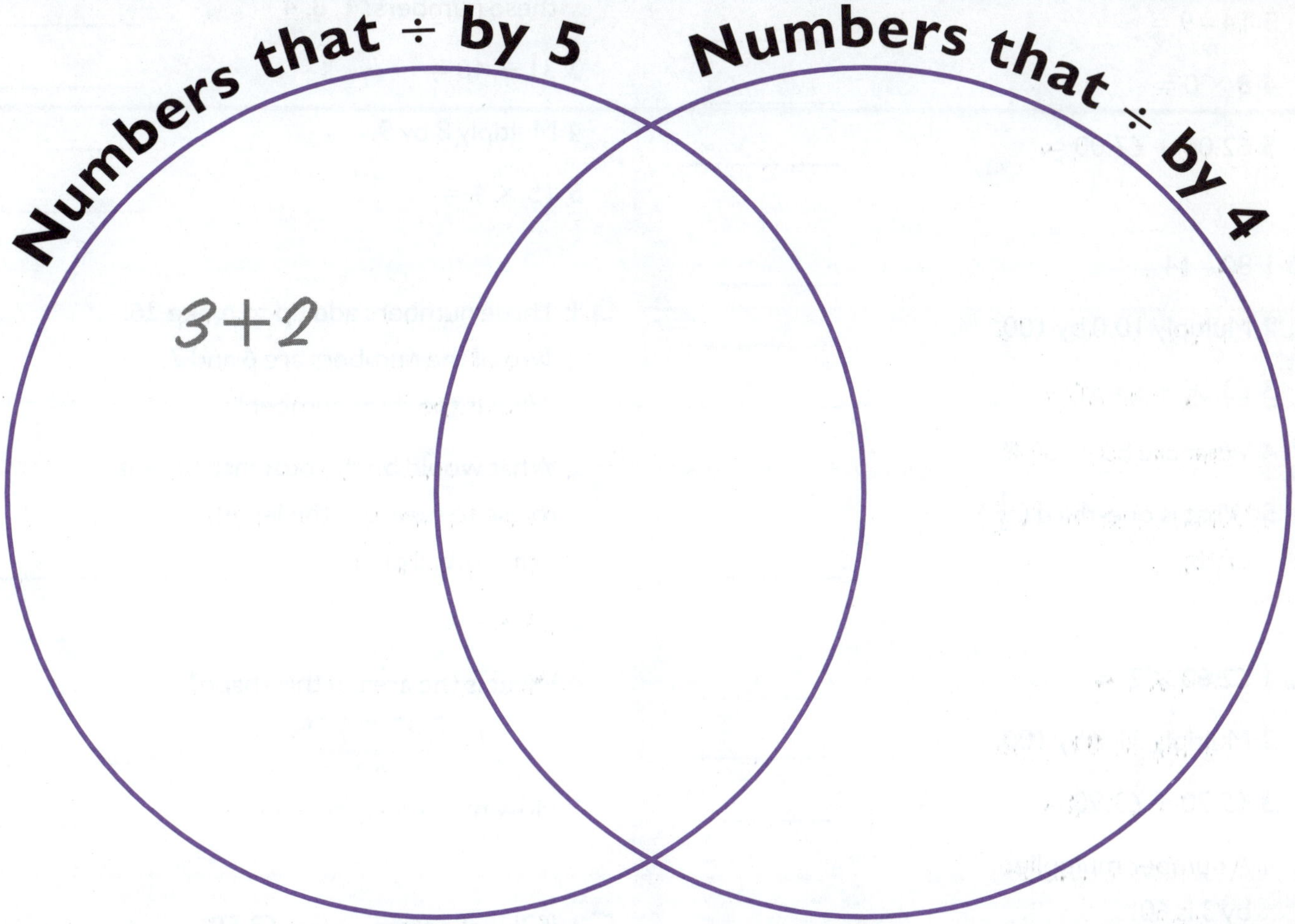

$16 + 19$ 5×2 3×8 $136 - 86$

~~$3 + 2$~~ 15×2 $47 - 7$ $37 - 9$

$18 + 2$ 4×4 $51 - 19$ 1×28

$18 - 3$ $300 \div 10$ $40 + 5 - 1$

Test 15

A 1 What is a quarter of 8? ______

2 3.5 × 10 = ______

3 14 – 9 = ______

4 8 × 0 = ______

5 £2.00 + £7.00 = ______

B 1 80 – 14 = ______

2 Multiply 10.0 by 100. ______

3 £3.80 + £3.30 = ______

4 What are 8 lots of 7? ______

5 What is one-third ($\frac{1}{3}$) of 18? ______

C 1 £2.60 × 2 = ______

2 Multiply 31.8 by 100. ______

3 £5.70 + £3.90 = ______

4 A number multiplied by 3 is 60. What is the number? ______

5 How much is $\frac{3}{5}$ of 30 minutes? ______

Test 16

A 1 36 × 10 = ______

2 What is the median of these numbers? 1, 8, 4 ______

3 31 + 46 = ______

4 Multiply 8 by 9. ______

5 15 × 4 = ______

B 1 Three numbers add up to make 26. Two of the numbers are 6 and 7. What is the third number? ______

2 What would be the best instrument to use to measure the length of a football pitch? ______

3 21 × 4 = ______

4 What is the area of this shape?

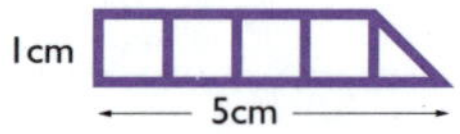

______

5 How much is 25% of 36? ______

C 1 If 7kg of potatoes cost £3.50, how much will 5kg cost? ______

2 £3.19 + £4.28 = ______

3 32 × 4 = ______

4 How many ml are there in 0.4 litres? ______

5 What is the volume of this box?

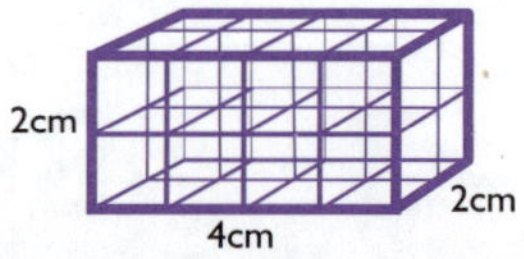

______

Helpful hints

It can be useful to multiply numbers larger than 10×10 in your head.

Here is how to do it.

Example: to multiply 17 by 9.

1 Multiply the 10 of 17 by 9 = 90 (remember the 90).

2 Multiply the 7 of 17 by 9 = 63.

3 Add together the 63 and the 90 which makes the answer: **153**.

The hard part is remembering the first answer while you work out the second answer.

Example: to multiply 23 by 8.

1 Multiply the 20 of 23 by 8 = 160 (remember the 160).

2 Multiply the 3 of 23 by 8 = 24.

3 Add together the 24 and the 160 which makes the answer: **184**.

Follow this example through:

16 x 7.

1 Multiply the 10 of 16 by 7 = 70 (remember the 70).

2 Multiply the 6 of 16 by 7 = 42.

3 Add together the 42 and the 70 which makes the answer: **112**.

Test 17

A 1 $13 \times 5 =$ ______

2 $18 \times 4 =$ ______

3 $15 \times 3 =$ ______

4 $17 \times 2 =$ ______

5 $19 \times 3 =$ ______

B 1 $16 \times 6 =$ ______

2 $17 \times 4 =$ ______

3 $18 \times 5 =$ ______

4 $14 \times 7 =$ ______

5 $13 \times 9 =$ ______

C 1 $17 \times 7 =$ ______

2 $16 \times 8 =$ ______

3 $18 \times 6 =$ ______

4 $15 \times 9 =$ ______

5 $19 \times 8 =$ ______

Test 18

A 1 What is the median of these numbers?
5, 2, 9 ________

2 How much is 50% of 18? ________

3 What is the result when 8 is multiplied by 5? ________

4 $14 \times 3 =$ ________

5 $70 - 20 =$ ________

B 1 What is the perimeter of a rectangle which is $\frac{1}{2}$cm wide and 3m long? ________

2 Write down all the factors of 6. ________

3 What is $\frac{1}{5}$ of £40? ________

4 $18 \times 5 =$ ________

5 Three numbers add up to 46.
Two of the numbers are 10 and 11.
What is the third number? ________

C 1 A rectangle has a perimeter of 20cm.
One side is 7cm, what length is the other side? ________

2 How many g are there in 0.5kg? ________

3 If 6 identical boxes weigh 42kg, how much will 8 boxes weigh? ________

4 £2.46 + £3.60 = ________

5 $31 \times 5 =$ ________

Test 19

A 1 50% of a number is 8.
What is the number? ________

2 $15 \times 5 =$ ________

3 What is $\frac{1}{2}$ of £18? ________

4 What is the mode of this group of numbers?
2, 4, 2, 1, 4, 2, 1 ________

5 $48 \div 6 =$ ________

B 1 Multiply £2.18 by 10. ________

2 $22 \times 4 =$ ________

3 Write down the first four multiples of 6. ________

4 Three sums of money add up to £40.
Two of the amounts are £8 and £6.
What is the third amount? ________

5 £5.00 – £1.63 = ________

C 1 75% of an amount is £150.
What is the amount? ________

2 £4.20 – £1.75 = ________

3 $26 \times 4 =$ ________

4 Each side of a regular octagon is 3.5cm long. What is the perimeter of the octagon? ________

5 What is the remainder when 70 is divided by 9? ________

Challenge 5

Connie can work out multiplication sums in her head like this.

25×7

a She multiplies 20 by 7 = 140

b Next she multiplies 5 by 7 = 35

c Finally she adds 140 and 35 = 175

Do these sums in the same way as Connie.

1 34×5

a Multiply 30 by 5 = ☐

b Multiply 4 by 5 = ☐

c Add ☐ and ☐ = ☐

2 29×3

a Multiply 20 by 3 = ☐

b Multiply 9 by 3 = ☐

c Add ☐ and ☐ = ☐

3 42×6

a Multiply 40 by 6 = ☐

b Multiply 2 by 6 = ☐

c Add ☐ and ☐ = ☐

4 51×6

a Multiply 50 by 6 = ☐

b Multiply 1 by 6 = ☐

c Add ☐ and ☐ = ☐

5 38×6

a Multiply 30 by 6 = ☐

b Multiply 8 by 6 = ☐

c Add ☐ and ☐ = ☐

6 35×5

a Multiply 30 by 5 = ☐

b Multiply 5 by 5 = ☐

c Add ☐ and ☐ = ☐

Challenge 6

Look carefully at these numbers and put them in order.

2145·3
21345
12345
24·5
23·5
243·5
135
1243·5
21435
1325·4
2314.5
2·3

Smallest first

___
___
___
___
___
___
___
___
___
___
___
___

Test 20

A 1 7p + 6p + 5p = ______

2 $7 \times 10 =$ ______

3 $8 \times 4 =$ ______

4 How much is $\frac{1}{2}$ of 20p? ______

5 Divide 35 by 7. ______

B 1 What are the factors of 8? ______

2 Divide £3.00 by 10. ______

3 If 7 stamps cost 63p, how much does each stamp cost? ______

4 What is 25% of 36? ______

5 £4.21 + £3.64 = ______

C 1 What number do these tally marks represent?
𝍸 𝍸 II ______

2 How much is three-quarters of £120? ______

3 What number multiplied by 6 gives an answer of 48? ______

4 Is it sensible to say that 0.3×100 is 30.0? ______

5 Divide 63 by 3. ______

Test 21

A 1 Multiply 5 by 6. ______

2 $40 \div 5 =$ ______

3 What is 50% of 18? ______

4 $8 \times 100 =$ ______

5 26p – 12p = ______

B 1 What is the median of these numbers?
2, 5, 3 ______

2 How much is $\frac{3}{4}$ of 20? ______

3 What is the remainder when 50 is divided by 6? ______

4 £2.60 – £1.28 = ______

5 Multiply 4 by 7. ______

C 1 What is 75% of 36? ______

2 Divide 24 by 10. ______

3 Show the number 9 as tally marks. ______

4 What is the area of this shape?

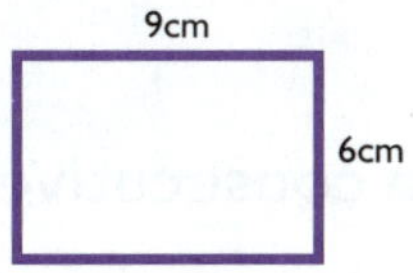

______

5 Which square number comes between 20 and 30? ______

Challenge 7

Consecutive numbers are numbers which are next to each other like 2 and 3 or 6 and 7.

If we multiply **2** by **3** we get **6**.
If we multiply **6** by **7** we get **42**.

1 Find two consecutive numbers that multiply together to make 20. ☐ and ☐

2 Find two consecutive numbers that multiply together to make 56. ☐ and ☐

3 Try to think of two consecutive numbers that multiply together to make 0. ☐ and ☐

4 Find three consecutive numbers that multiply to make 60. ☐, ☐ and ☐

5 Find three consecutive numbers that multiply together to make 120. ☐, ☐ and ☐

6 Find three consecutive numbers that multiply together to make 720. ☐, ☐ and ☐

Helpful hints

You will sometimes need to work out sums quickly and still get them right.

If you have sums to do quickly, go through them answering the easier ones first and then come back to the harder ones. It is often a mistake to go through them in order.

Try to answer these questions as quickly as possible. Sometimes you will find most of them are easy but one is harder than the others.

If this happens, come back to the harder questions when you have finished the others and try again.

Test 22

1 3 × 2 = ______

2 4 × 5 = ______

3 2 × 6 = ______

4 9 × 2 = ______

5 10 × 4 = ______

6 3 × 3 = ______

7 8 × 1 = ______

8 2 × 4 = ______

9 3 × 10 = ______

10 1 × 5 = ______

Test 23

Try to answer each group of questions in 30 seconds or less.

A 1 3 + 3 + 3 = ______

2 4 + 2 + 1 = ______

3 8 + 6 + 5 = ______

4 1 + 3 + 5 = ______

5 6 + 1 + 0 = ______

B 1 12 − 8 = ______

2 23 − 15 = ______

3 13 − 7 = ______

4 10 − 4 = ______

5 15 − 6 = ______

C 1 9 × 8 = ______

2 6 × 4 = ______

3 5 × 4 = ______

4 8 × 5 = ______

5 10 × 6 = ______

Test 24

Try to answer each section in 30 seconds or less.

A 1 £10 × 3 = ______

2 £100 × 8 = ______

3 £147 × 100 = ______

4 £32 × 10 = ______

5 £10 × 50 = ______

B 1 £1.50 + £1.50 = ______

2 £3.20 + £4.60 = ______

3 £2.00 + £3.75 = ______

4 £5.00 − £1.25 = ______

5 £3.50 − £1.30 = ______

C 1 £1.25 × 2 = ______

2 £1.75 × 3 = ______

3 £2.50 × 2 = ______

4 £3.00 × 10 = ______

5 £1.50 × 3 = ______

Test 25

Try to answer each section in 30 seconds or less.

A 1 50% of 10 = ______

2 50% of 11 = ______

3 50% of 6 = ______

4 50% of 4 = ______

5 50% of 8 = ______

B 1 25% of 12 = ______

2 25% of 8 = ______

3 25% of 36 = ______

4 25% of 20 = ______

5 25% of 4 = ______

C 1 75% of 20 = ______

2 75% of 120 = ______

3 75% of 12 = ______

4 75% of 40 = ______

5 75% of 8 = ______

Test 26

Try to answer each section in 30 seconds or less.

A 1 $\frac{1}{2}$ of 6 = ______

2 $\frac{1}{2}$ of 18 = ______

3 $\frac{1}{2}$ of 4 = ______

4 $\frac{1}{2}$ of 8 = ______

5 $\frac{1}{2}$ of 2 = ______

B 1 $\frac{1}{4}$ of 12 = ______

2 $\frac{1}{4}$ of 32 = ______

3 $\frac{1}{4}$ of 4 = ______

4 $\frac{1}{4}$ of 40 = ______

5 $\frac{1}{4}$ of 16 = ______

C 1 $\frac{3}{4}$ of 8 = ______

2 $\frac{3}{4}$ of 36 = ______

3 $\frac{3}{4}$ of 12 = ______

4 $\frac{3}{4}$ of 100 = ______

5 $\frac{3}{4}$ of 28 = ______

Test 27

Try to answer each section in 30 seconds or less.

A 1 $3\overline{)9}$ ______

2 $4\overline{)36}$ ______

3 $5\overline{)10}$ ______

4 $2\overline{)12}$ ______

5 $3\overline{)15}$ ______

B 1 $18 \div 3 =$ ______

2 $24 \div 6 =$ ______

3 $56 \div 7 =$ ______

4 $30 \div 5 =$ ______

5 $24 \div 2 =$ ______

C 1 $81 \div 9 =$ ______

2 $63 \div 7 =$ ______

3 $48 \div 6 =$ ______

4 $45 \div 3 =$ ______

5 $60 \div 2 =$ ______

Challenge 8

Complete each series.

1	7 × 10 →	70	×100 →	7000	×1000 →	7000000
2	23 × 10 →		×100 →		×1000 →	
3	19 × 10 →		×100 →		÷1000 →	
4	124 × 10 →		×100 →		÷1000 →	
5	530 ÷ 10 →		×1000 →		÷10 →	
6	38 × 100 →		×10 →		÷1000 →	
7	9 × 1000 →		÷10 →		×100 →	
8	400 ÷ 100 →		×1000 →		÷10 →	
9	26 × 1000 →		÷10 →		×100 →	
10	8000 ÷ 1000 →		×10 →		÷100 →	

Challenge 9

Some of these sentences are true but some are not.
Put a *T* (true) or *F* (false) in each box.

1 A half of 18 is the same as 50% of 18. ☐

2 25% of 20 is the same as a quarter of 20. ☐

3 A half of 24 is the same as 25% of 40. ☐

4 50% of 100 is equal to 25% of 80. ☐

5 100% of 15 is equal to 50% of 30. ☐

6 25% of a metre is the same as 25cm. ☐

7 75% of £2.00 is the same as $\frac{1}{2}$ of £3.00. ☐

8 Three-quarters of 20 is the same as 25% of 40. ☐

9 A half of 9 is the same as 25% of 18. ☐

10 25% of £5.00 is equal to 50% of £10.00. ☐

Make your own true sentences, starting with these parts.

1 A half of 24 is the same as ☐ % of 48.

2 50% of 200ml is the same as a $\frac{1}{4}$ of ☐ ml.

3 Three-quarters of 100 is the same as ☐ of 150.

Test 28

A 1 What is 50% of 10?

2 Divide 48 by 6.

3 34p + 14p =

4 Multiply 10 by 12.

5 What is $\frac{1}{2}$ of 16cm?

B 1 £1.44 + £1.27 =

2 What is the median of these numbers? 18, 16, 14

3 What is the area of this shape?

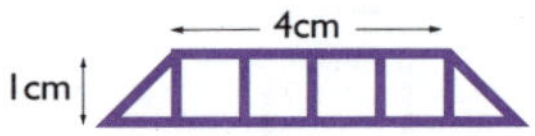

4 Multiply three by eight.

5 What is the remainder when 26 is divided by 3?

C 1 Which square number comes between 60 and 70?

2 What is the median of these numbers? 3, 4, 7, 2 and 5

3 Divide 63 by 10.

4 One-third of a number is 9. What is the number?

5 What is the volume of a box which has a square base, a side of 2cm and a height of 3cm?

Test 29

A 1 What is $\frac{1}{2}$ of £3.00?

2 Multiply 15 by 10.

3 46p + 26p =

4 40 ÷ 10 =

5 Divide 56 by 7.

B 1 Add £2.24 and £2.36.

2 What is 25% of 80?

3 Divide 7300 by 10.

4 Write down all the factors of 4.

5 What is the perimeter of this shape?

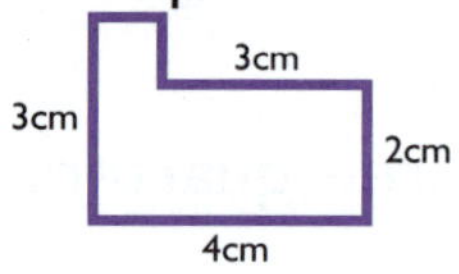

C 1 Divide 48 by 4.

2 75% of a number is 15. What is the number?

3 Which number comes next? 1, 3, 9, ____

4 What is two-thirds of 15?

5 A number multiplied by 7 is 42. What is the number?

Test 30

A 1 $4 \times 7 =$ ______

2 Divide 24 by 3. ______

3 $10 \times 17 =$ ______

4 $31p + 29p =$ ______

5 50% of a number is 4.
What is the number? ______

B 1 What is the remainder when
42 is divided by 5? ______

2 Add £3.90 to £1.30. ______

3 What is the median of these numbers?
5, 8, 4, 1, 3 ______

4 How much is $\frac{3}{4}$ of £1.00? ______

5 Divide 6000 by 100. ______

C 1 A regular shape has sides that are 6cm
long and its perimeter is 30cm.
What is the shape? ______

2 Which is the next
square number after 49? ______

3 What is the total of 6.24 and 3.47? ______

4 A number multiplied by 9 gives 72.
What is the number? ______

5 Three-quarters of a number is 27.
What is the number? ______

Test 31

A 1 What is $\frac{1}{2}$ of 50p? ______

2 $30 \times 100 =$ ______

3 Take 13p from 50p. ______

4 $6 \times 4 =$ ______

5 What is the perimeter
of this
shape? ______

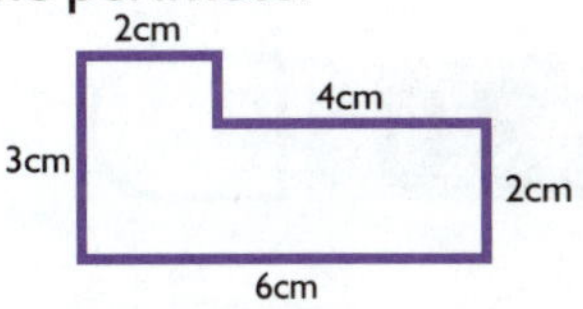

B 1 25% of a number is 8.
What is the number? ______

2 What is one-quarter of 36p? ______

3 What is the remainder when 63
is divided by 10? ______

4 Add £5.67 to £3.21. ______

5 What is the median of these numbers?
30, 20, 31 ______

C 1 A box is 4cm long, 3cm wide and
3cm high. What is its volume? ______

2 Write down all the factors of 31.
______

3 Which square number
comes before 9? ______

4 What number comes next?
100, 10, 1, ______

5 What number gives 54
when multiplied by 6? ______

Challenge 10

James knows that to find $\frac{2}{3}$ of a number he must first find $\frac{1}{3}$ and then multiply by 2.

Find $\frac{2}{3}$ of each amount:

9 ☐

30 ☐

21 ☐

99 ☐

12 ☐

60 ☐

James knows that each of these numbers is $\frac{2}{3}$ of a whole number.
What is each whole number?

4 ☐

16 ☐

20 ☐

These numbers are $\frac{3}{4}$ of whole numbers.
What is each whole number?

15 ☐

30 ☐

21 ☐

Test 32

A 1 Put these numbers in order, starting with the smallest first.
6, −4, 5, −2 ______

2 7 × 1000 = ______

3 4 − 5 = ______

4 7.4 + 1.7 = ______

5 What is one-third of £24.00? ______

B 1 Is an acute angle bigger or smaller than an obtuse angle? ______

2 Divide 10 litres by 1000. ______

3 16 × 1000 = ______

4 Multiply 23 by 3. ______

5 4.30 − 1.70 = ______

C 1 Divide 8.5 litres by 1000. ______

2 Add 3.72km and 1.69km. ______

3 A child's building brick weighs 0.8g. How much will 20 weigh? ______

4 What size is angle *x*?

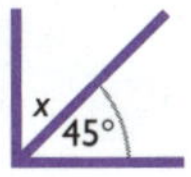

______

5 53 × 5 = ______

Test 33

A 1 9 × 1000 = ______

2 How many degrees are there in half a right angle? ______

3 3.4 + 2.5 = ______

4 What is 25% of £200? ______

5 Add 32 and 18. ______

B 1 Divide £5.70 by 3. ______

2 26 × 1000 = ______

3 Multiply £1.20 by 4. ______

4 −6 − 48 = ______

5 Add £1.20, £0.75 and £1.35. ______

C 1 A cup holds 0.62 litres of water. How much would 8 cups hold? ______

2 Divide 3600 by 1000. ______

3 How many lines of symmetry does a regular hexagon have? ______

4 Three pairs of identical shoes cost £37.50. How much does each pair cost? ______

5 263 × 100 = ______

Test yourself 1

1 £4.00 – £1.50 = __________

2 What is 25% of £1.00? __________

3 Divide 900 by 10. __________

4 $23 \times 100 =$ __________

5 Which number comes next? 7, 14, 21, __________

6 What is the perimeter of a rectangle with sides of 5cm and 6cm? __________

7 38p + 40p = __________

8 How much change will you have from £5.00 if you spend £2.26? __________

9 $6 \times 6 =$ __________

10 What is half of 60? __________

11 How many minutes are there between 1:45 and 2:20? __________

12 Add 46cm and 54cm. __________

13 Half of a number is 32. What is the number? __________

14 How many cm are there in a quarter of a metre? __________

15 Double 58. __________

16 Multiply 8 by 4. __________

17 63 – 14 = __________

18 £2.26 + £3.32 = __________

19 What is $\frac{1}{3}$ of 15? __________

20 What are 8 lots of 7? __________

Test yourself 2

1 Multiply 7 by 6. ____________

2 $70 - 12 =$ ____________

3 £3.76 + £2.28 = ____________

4 3 identical boxes weigh 21kg. How much does each box weigh? ____________

5 $21 \times 3 =$ ____________

6 31p + 47p = ____________

7 What is 25% of 60? ____________

8 Double 64. ____________

9 If 6 stamps cost 54p, how much does each stamp cost? ____________

10 What is the remainder when 50 is divided by 7? ____________

11 $67 \times 100 =$ ____________

12 What is $\frac{3}{4}$ of 8? ____________

13 What are the factors of 10? ________________________

14 Subtract £2.26 from £3.00. ____________

15 Multiply £1.20 by 4. ____________

16 What is the median of these numbers? 12, 9, 15 ____________

17 What is 25% of 200cm? ____________

18 What is 380 divided by 10? ____________

19 $-5 - 36 =$ ____________

20 $6.0 + 1.7 =$ ____________

Answers

Test 1 **A 1** 7 **2** 150 **3** £10.00 **4** £1.00 **5** 22cm
B 1 £64 **2** £2.50 **3** 170 **4** 5 r 1 or $5\frac{1}{8}$ **5** 18p
C 1 260 **2** £7.80 **3** 21 **4** 60 **5** £2.20

Test 2 **A 1** 33 **2** 10cm **3** 36 **4** 75p **5** 20
B 1 £3.05 **2** 1800 **3** 100cm (1 m) **4** 56 **5** 40
C 1 40p **2** 13p **3** 2500g **4** 144cm^2 **5** 60

Test 3 **A 1** £2.40 **2** £1.60 **3** £0.20 or 20p **4** £0.90 or 90p
B 1 £3.25 **2** £3.65 **3** £4.15 **4** £2.75
C 1 £3.27 **2** £1.49 **3** £4.91 **4** £8.58

Test 4 **A 1** 76 **2** 3 **3** 6 **4** 100 **5** 18cm
B 1 81 **2** £3.75 **3** £7.00 **4** 3200 **5** 40
C 1 28p **2** 72 **3** 5 **4** £6.00 **5** 26cm^2

Test 5 **A 1** 7 **2** 140 **3** 40 **4** 80p or £0.80 **5** 75
B 1 £5 **2** 8p **3** 20 **4** 42 **5** 12cm
C 1 £5.78 **2** £2.50 **3** 1, 2, 3, 6, 9, 18 **4** 2 **5** 32

Challenge 1
1 6 **2** 6 **3** 100 **4** 8 **5** 7 **6** 4 **7** 1000 **8** 32

Test 6 **A 1** 3 **2** 20p or £0.20 **3** £2.50 **4** 40 **5** £2.70
B 1 1 **2** £6.00 **3** 70 **4** 4cm **5** £5000
C 1 £11.69 **2** £1.80 **3** 1000 **4** 5cm **5** 1, 2, 4, 5, 10, 20

Test 7 **A 1** 21 **2** 200 **3** 40cm **4** 30 **5** 9
B 1 4 **2** 4 **3** £6.67 **4** £0.55 or 55p **5** 52
C 1 £6.50 **2** £1.25 **3** 68cm **4** 9cm **5** 92

Test 8 **A 1** 60.0 **2** 90.0 **3** 30.0 **4** 45.0 **5** 75.0
B 1 310.0 **2** 580.0 **3** 125.0 **4** 212.0 **5** 102.0
C 1 1360.0 **2** 80.0 **3** 422.0 **4** 2.0 **5** 13020.0

Challenge 2

Column 1	Column 2	Column 3
2.6	1.3	3.9
3.2	2.5	5.7
1.8	2.8	4.6
4.6	5.2	9.8
3.4	1.8	5.2
9.5	0.3	9.8
4.6	2.7	7.3
5.4	3.7	9.1
3.7	3.9	7.6
6.2	1.9	8.1

Test 9 **A 1** 30.0 **2** 20 **3** 6 **4** £5.00 **5** 11
B 1 6 **2** 69.0 **3** £4.70 **4** 9 **5** 81
C 1 64 **2** 12 **3** 60.0 **4** £3.28 **5** £5.65

Test 10 **A 1** 3 **2** 24 **3** 9 **4** 40.0 **5** £4.00
B 1 14 **2** 42 **3** 8 **4** 710.0 **5** £3.70
C 1 £0.72 or 72p **2** 56p **3** 14 **4** £5.33 **5** 11.0

Test 11 **A 1** 50p or £0.50 **2** 30.0 **3** £6.50 **4** 5 **5** 15
B 1 9 **2** 58.0 **3** £8.70 **4** 18 **5** 21
C 1 3610.0 **2** 5 **3** £1.91 **4** £36 **5** £1.87

Test 12 **A 1** £1.50 **2** 16 **3** 50cm or 0.5m **4** 800.0 **5** 6
B 1 21 **2** 19 **3** 490.0 **4** 7 **5** £2.60
C 1 2 **2** £2.92 **3** 602.0 **4** £1.55 **5** £30

Test 13 **A 1** 16 **2** 7 **3** £5.55 **4** 100.0 **5** 7
B 1 £2.75 **2** 87.0 **3** 500ml **4** 70 **5** 22
C 1 48 **2** 20p or £0.20 **3** £3.90 **4** 24p **5** 3030.0

Test 14 **A 1** £2.50 **2** 10 **3** 50.0 **4** 21 **5** 5
B 1 48 **2** £1.50 **3** 19 **4** £2.30 **5** 122.0
C 1 £2.62 **2** 88p **3** 620.0cm **4** 40cm (0.4m) **5** 42

Challenge 3

6	**10**	**18**	**21**	**29**	**36**
1, 2, 3, 6	1, 2, 5, 10	1, 2, 3, 6, 9, 18	1, 3, 7, 21	1, 29	1, 2, 3, 4, 6, 9, 12, 18, 36

42	**49**	**55**	**80**
1, 2, 3, 6, 7, 14, 21, 42	1, 7, 49	1, 5, 11, 55	1, 2, 4, 5, 8, 10, 16, 20, 40, 80

Challenge 4

Numbers that ÷ by 5	Numbers that ÷ by 5 and ÷ by 4	Numbers that ÷ by 4
16 + 19 = 35	18 + 2 = 20	3 x 8 = 24
18 – 3 = 15	47 – 7 = 40	37 – 9 = 28
15 x 2 = 30		4 x 4 = 16
5 x 2 = 10		1 x 28 = 28
136 – 86 = 50		51 – 19 = 32
300 ÷ 10 = 30		40 + 5 – 1 = 44
3 + 2 = 5		

Test 15 **A 1** 2 **2** 35.0 **3** 5 **4** 0 **5** £9.00
B 1 66 **2** 1000.0 **3** £7.10 **4** 56 **5** 6
C 1 £5.20 **2** 3180.0 **3** £9.60 **4** 20 **5** 18 minutes

Test 16 **A 1** 360 **2** 4 **3** 77 **4** 72 **5** 60
B 1 13 **2** metre stick/click wheel/trundle wheel **3** 84 **4** $4\frac{1}{2}$cm^2 or 4.5cm^2 **5** 9
C 1 £2.50 **2** £7.47 **3** 128 **4** 400ml **5** 16cm^3

Test 17 **A 1** 65 **2** 72 **3** 45 **4** 34 **5** 57
B 1 96 **2** 68 **3** 90 **4** 98 **5** 117
C 1 119 **2** 128 **3** 108 **4** 135 **5** 152

Test 18 **A 1** 5 **2** 9 **3** 40 **4** 42 **5** 50
B 1 601cm or 6.01m **2** 1, 2, 3, 6 **3** £8 **4** 90 **5** 25
C 1 3cm **2** 500g **3** 56kg **4** £6.06 **5** 155

Test 19 **A 1** 16 **2** 75 **3** £9 **4** 2 **5** 8
B 1 £21.80 **2** 88 **3** 6, 12, 18, 24 **4** £26 **5** £3.37
C 1 £200 **2** £2.45 **3** 104 **4** 28cm **5** 7

Challenge 5
1 a 150 **b** 20 **c** 150, 20, 170
2 a 60 **b** 27 **c** 60, 27, 87
3 a 240 **b** 12 **c** 240, 12, 252
4 a 300 **b** 6 **c** 300, 6, 306
5 a 180 **b** 48 **c** 180, 48, 228
6 a 150 **b** 25 **c** 150, 25, 175

Challenge 6
2.3 23.5 24.5 135 243.5 1243.5 1325.4 2145.3 2314.5 12345 21345 21435

Test 20 **A 1** 18p **2** 70 **3** 32 **4** 10p **5** 5
B 1 1, 2, 4, 8 **2** 30p or £0.30 **3** 9p **4** 9 **5** £7.85
C 1 12 **2** £90 **3** 8 **4** yes **5** 21

Test 21 **A 1** 30 **2** 8 **3** 9 **4** 800 **5** 14p
B 1 3 **2** 15 **3** 2 **4** £1.32 **5** 28
C 1 27 **2** 2.4 **3** 卌|||| **4** 54cm^2 **5** 25

Challenge 7
1 4 and 5 **2** 7 and 8 **3** 0 and 1
4 3, 4 and 5 **5** 4, 5 and 6 **6** 8, 9 and 10

Test 22 **1** 6 **2** 20 **3** 12 **4** 18 **5** 40 **6** 9 **7** 8 **8** 8 **9** 30 **10** 5

Test 23 **A 1** 9 **2** 7 **3** 19 **4** 9 **5** 7
B 1 4 **2** 8 **3** 6 **4** 6 **5** 9
C 1 72 **2** 24 **3** 20 **4** 40 **5** 60

Test 24 **A 1** £30 **2** £800 **3** £14700 **4** £320 **5** £500
B 1 £3.00 **2** £7.80 **3** £5.75 **4** £3.75 **5** £2.20
C 1 £2.50 **2** £5.25 **3** £5.00 **4** £30.00 **5** £4.50

Test 25 **A 1** 5 **2** $5\frac{1}{2}$ (5.5) **3** 3 **4** 2 **5** 4
B 1 3 **2** 2 **3** 9 **4** 5 **5** 1
C 1 15 **2** 90 **3** 9 **4** 30 **5** 6

Test 26 **A 1** 3 **2** 9 **3** 2 **4** 4 **5** 1
B 1 3 **2** 8 **3** 1 **4** 10 **5** 4
C 1 6 **2** 27 **3** 9 **4** 75 **5** 21

Test 27 **A 1** 3 **2** 9 **3** 2 **4** 6 **5** 5
B 1 6 **2** 4 **3** 8 **4** 6 **5** 12
C 1 9 **2** 9 **3** 8 **4** 15 **5** 30

Challenge 8

1	70	7000	7 000 000	**6**	3800	38 000	38
2	230	23 000	23 000 000	**7**	9000	900	90 000
3	190	19 000	19	**8**	4	4000	400
4	1240	124 000	124	**9**	26 000	2600	260 000
5	53	53 000	5300	**10**	8	80	0.8

Challenge 9
1 T **2** T **3** F **4** F **5** T **6** T **7** T **8** F **9** T **10** F
1 25% **2** 400 ml **3** $\frac{1}{2}$ or 50%

Test 28 **A 1** 5 **2** 8 **3** 48p **4** 120 **5** 8cm
B 1 £2.71 **2** 16 **3** 5cm^2 **4** 24 **5** 2
C 1 64 **2** 4 **3** 6.3 **4** 27 **5** 12cm^3

Test 29 **A 1** £1.50 **2** 150 **3** 72p **4** 4 **5** 8
B 1 £4.60 **2** 20 **3** 730 **4** 1, 2, 4 **5** 14cm
C 1 12 **2** 20 **3** 27 **4** 10 **5** 6

Test 30 **A 1** 28 **2** 8 **3** 170 **4** 60p **5** 8
B 1 2 **2** £5.20 **3** 4 **4** 75p or £0.75 **5** 60
C 1 pentagon **2** 64 **3** 9.71 **4** 8 **5** 36

Test 31 **A 1** 25p **2** 3000 **3** 37p **4** 24 **5** 18cm
B 1 32 **2** 9p **3** 3 **4** £8.88 **5** 30
C 1 36cm^3 **2** 1, 31 **3** 4 **4** 0.1 **5** 9

Challenge 10
20, 6, 14, 8, 40, 66 6, 30, 24 20, 40, 28

Test 32 **A 1** –4, –2, 5, 6 **2** 7000 **3** –1 **4** 9.1 **5** £8.00
B 1 smaller **2** 10 ml or 0.01 litres **3** 16 000 **4** 69 **5** 2.60
C 1 8.5 ml or 0.0085 litres **2** 5.41km **3** 16g **4** 45° **5** 265

Test 33 **A 1** 9000 **2** 45° **3** 5.9 **4** £50 **5** 50
B 1 £1.90 **2** 26 000 **3** £4.80 **4** –54 **5** £3.30
C 1 4.96 litres **2** 3.6 **3** 6 **4** £12.50 **5** 26 300

Test yourself 1
1 £2.50 **2** £0.25 or 25p **3** 90 **4** 2300 **5** 28 **6** 22cm **7** 78p **8** £2.74
9 36 **10** 30 **11** 35 minutes **12** 100cm or 1m **13** 64 **14** 25cm **15** 116
16 32 **17** 49 **18** £5.58 **19** 5 **20** 56

Test yourself 2
1 42 **2** 58 **3** £6.04 **4** 7kg **5** 63 **6** 78p **7** 15 **8** 128 **9** 9p
10 1 **11** 6700 **12** 6 **13** 1, 2, 5, 10 **14** £0.74 or 74p **15** £4.80 **16** 12
17 50cm **18** 38 **19** –41 **20** 7.7